MAT

UNDERSTANDING
Your 2 Year Old

The Tavistock Clinic, London, was founded in 1920, in order to meet the needs of people whose lives had been disrupted by the First World War. Today, it is still committed to understanding people's needs though, of course, times and people have changed. Now, as well as working with adults and adolescents, the Tavistock Clinic has a large department for children and families. This offers help to parents who are finding the challenging task of bringing up their children daunting and has, therefore, a wide experience of children of all ages. It is firmly committed to early intervention in the inevitable problems that arise as children grow up, and to the view that if difficulties are caught early enough, parents are the best people to help their children with them.

Professional Staff of the Clinic were, therefore, pleased to be able to contribute to this series of books to describe the ordinary development of children, to help in spotting the growing pains and to provide ways that parents might think about their children's growth.

Susan Reid worked as a teacher after leaving Sheffield University. She went to the Tavistock Clinic in 1970 to train as a child psychotherapist and has continued to work there ever since. She is based in the Child and Family Department where her time is divided between clinical work, research and the training of child psychotherapists. She lectures in Europe and America and her publications include "The Importance of Beauty in the Psychoanalytical Experience", Tavistock Clinic, 1987.

Susan Reid is married with two teenagers and has recently had another baby.

UNDERSTANDING
Your 2 year old

Susan Reid

of the

TAVISTOCK CLINIC

Series Editor: Elsie Osborne

ROSENDALE PRESS

First published in Great Britain in 1992 by:
Rosendale Press Ltd.
Premier House, 10 Greycoat Place
London SW1P 1SB

Design by Pep Reiff
Production Edward Allhusen
Typesetting Ace Filmsetting Ltd
Printed in the United Kingdom by Redwood Press

British Library Cataloguing in Publication Data
A catalogue record for this book is available from
The British Library

ISBN 1 872803 15 6

CONTENTS

INTRODUCTION

The change from birth to two years is the most stunning period of change and development in a human being's lifespan. The move from a totally dependent baby to the walking, talking, running, playing, thinking, reasoning, unreasonable two year old can make us, as parents, lose a sense of perspective. Between two and three the child can do so much of what the grown-up can do that it is all too easy to become unreasonable in our expectations, to treat them as short adults!

It can be such a shock in later years to see a photo, or video perhaps, of our child at two; looking back down the years they seem so small, not much more than babies, and we can be shaken to remember what we expected of them.

When our child is two, however, what we are struck by is the change from the baby to the little person we live with now, so much more recognizably like ourselves than the baby. A two year old can talk with increasing fluency, have a conversation, have opinions, ask endless questions, can argue and answer back and make a bid for independence.

Two year olds question all the time and this is not a bad model; bringing up a two year old is much more rewarding when we try to understand the meaning of what they do and question our own responses.

This very bid for independence when the child is between two and three also confuses us. If we constantly over-estimate his or her capacities, the child is busy doing the same. When a child seems able to do so much it's hard for us to remember how little they really know about the world; what a mystery much of it must still be. Under pressure the two year old quickly becomes a baby who still needs an "umbilical cord"; a mental connectedness to mother.

The discovery of the mysteries and beauty of the world is what makes living with the two year old such a source of pleasure to parents. What an exciting, beautiful, frustrating, puzzling, baffling and frightening place it is. The two year old's observations are frequently truly delightful and charming, often amusing, and frequently give us cause to look at the familiar in a fresh way.

Some parents enjoy this phase of their child's life more than the dependence of the first two years: they are reassured that the child has "survived" (a fear all parents have at some level even when their baby is healthy); relieved by his or her growing independence; reassured by the child's increasing capacities which are demonstrated all the time, each day brings something new. Some parents find it much easier to relate to a child with language, a child they can have a conversation with.

Other parents wonder where that lovely, dependent little thing has gone; they relished being needed all the time and feel irritated by the two year old's bids for independence which can feel "against mummy or daddy".

Most parents probably fall somewhere in between. Few

can fail to be charmed some of the time and infuriated at others. This new phase of their child's life can also be a second chance for some parents and babies who didn't get off to a very good start.

The task of this book, like the others in the series, is not to give advice but to help parents to think through situations most parents of two year olds encounter, so that they may then find an effective answer for their child. To this end each section is illustrated by examples taken from the lives of two year olds and their families. In reading this book, with the examples given, parents may find another perspective from which to observe their child.

No two year olds are the same but all are alike. If they all needed exactly the same, then bringing up children would be a very easy task – we could simply follow a prescription. The examples give individual children's reactions to particular situations; some of them may feel immediately recognizable to you; others, perhaps not at all. The examples taken are from families from different social classes, and different ethnic groups. Although differences are important and a potential source of richness, it is the similarities in the two year old's experiences of the world and what seems to help the two year old to grow into a happy, secure individual, which are the focus in this book.

Your child at two years one month will also be very different from your child at two years eleven months. Each child will have his or her own unique personality and rate of development. Even identical twins have different personalities. Some two year olds speak fluently when only just two, others are much nearer to being three before this occurs. The child who talks fluently may not be as agile or physically bold. Of course all parents seem to know of a two year old who manages the lot and causes other parents no end of concern and competitiveness! It's worth knowing, if this is your first child, that within another year it doesn't really seem to matter much whether the child spoke fluently at two, two and a half, or nearly three: you probably will no longer remember with any degree of certainty. Only if your child is behind in all respects, and doesn't seem to be enjoying contact with you and others, is there cause for concern and the need to consult professionals.

So this is not a book about child care, but about how the mind and personality of the two year old grows; what they understand of the world in which they live and how, as parents, we can enhance this. The aim is to take you, as parents, back into the world the two year old inhabits. When you rediscover that world which you left behind long ago, then you can see the world as your child sees it and this helps you as the adult to keep in mind that 2 year olds are on the boundary of babyhood and childhood. This recognition greatly enhances the potential for communication and thus for harmony in the family.

So much has happened by the time the child is two that we often feel we've been through a life-time together – which in some sense is true. The early years provide the all important foundations for future development.

Having a two year old is pleasure but also very, very hard work and another aim of this book is to help parents sort out what is realizable for them from what is "ideal". If we set ourselves achievable goals then we are more likely to enjoy being a parent. If we can be generous and reasonable with ourselves there is also more chance that we will set our two year old realizable goals too. We need to keep a careful eye on ourselves for when we are getting over-tired and need a break. Here, too, realizable goals are important: just to go to the shops without the two year old can feel like a small holiday. It doesn't have to be something big, like an evening out, which isn't always easy to arrange, but important still to manage from time to time. Time away, providing it's not for too long, leaves the grown-ups refreshed.

Refreshed parents are better able to keep a helpful adult eye on the two year old, to remember who the real adult is. Two year olds are excited by their powers and so they should be, but a careful eye is needed because they can so easily over-reach themselves and get into dangerous situations, both physically, and emotionally. We need to be able to judge when the two year old has collapsed and become, temporarily, a dependent, clinging baby again before being ready, with parents' help, to take on the world once more.

UNDERSTANDING YOUR CHILD

Loving the child you've got

You may have wanted a boy and got a girl or vice versa. We can't choose the child we want and there is an element of luck in whether we have the child whose personality suits us. The same child is seen quite differently by different people: a child described as full of life by one family can be seen as hyperactive by another. By the time their child is two most parents have got over any disappointments and settled down to the pleasures and pains of living with the child they've got. By now also they will have some conviction about the kind of child they have. Easy going, friendly, shy, nervous, very sensitive, tough and so on. What seems to matter is if parents can enjoy the mystery and excitement of allowing their child to become whatever they seem destined to be. Parents can provide a helpful, accepting, sustaining setting in which this can take place. Sometimes nature seems to have created a bit of a mis-match, but some of the most successful marriages are where opposites come together.

Take Becky; by two it was apparent that she was a very feminine little girl, "a text-book girl" her mother affectionately called her. Whilst some of her features were recognizably her mother's and some her father's, she didn't really look much like either of them. Becky was tiny and delicate, her movements graceful. She heartily disliked any rough play and loved doing quiet absorbing activities which required considerable concentration. She was strong minded and quickly showed a preference for dresses over trousers and loved to wear a bracelet or carry a little handbag. Her mother, Anna, favoured trousers and in truth was never to be seen in a skirt. Large boned, handsome rather than pretty, she was a sporty, active person. She was a strong feminist and at first she seemed quite thrown by her feminine little daughter, and commented on how unlike herself she was. However, Anna is a warm, humorous person and soon began to recognise in Becky's strong will and determination a link with herself. As time went on she took affectionate and amused pride in Becky, respecting the strength of character that made her uniquely "her own woman". This seemed to calm Anna's fears that "feminine" automatically meant docile and subservient. Becky showed this was clearly not the case. So by two and a half Becky wore dresses most of the time and acquired a selection of handbags while the other little girls of their acquaintance seemed more at home in trousers.

A difficult start in life

Claudia was premature and her birth was difficult. As a new baby she cried a lot and was often sick. She was timid, her mother felt, and was easily startled.

Quiet support and containment can do much to change a bad start. Claudia's mother seemed to understand her daughter and not expect her to be like everyone else.

Silvia and Claudia belonged to a very supportive mother and baby group which met regularly in each other's homes and shared outings and activities such as trips to the park, and, when the children were all between two and three they went to the local swimming pool to introduce them to the water. There was a small warm pool for babies and young children.

Five mothers and their two year olds shared this new adventure. Two of the children went into the water immediately, held by their mothers at first but soon bobbing up and down with arm bands on. Two others clung to their mothers for a while but soon began to enjoy themselves, jumping up and down in the warm pool water, the children smacking the water with their little hands, looking suspicious when the water splashed their faces, but recovering quickly. David even recovered after a coughing fit when a swell of water submerged his head.

But Claudia screamed from the second her mother brought her to the water. She clutched at her mother as for dear life, threw back her head and howled. Silvia wrapped her in a towel and walked away from the water to a bench at the side. Silvia tried to talk to Claudia about her little friends in the water but Claudia screamed so loudly that her mother's voice was drowned. After about ten minutes Claudia calmed and Silvia tried again. But again Claudia screamed, making such a noise that her little friends looked up in alarm and had to be reassured by their own mothers. Silvia could have been embarrassed by this, but if she was she showed no sign of it. Back she went to the seat to calm Claudia. Silvia began to feel extremely cold – she had not brought a towel for herself. A friend offered to fetch her towel and she gratefully accepted, feeling perhaps the support of the friend through this gesture. Silvia's handling of Claudia was greatly respected by the other adults, several of whom openly admitted that they did not have the patience and tenacity which Silvia demonstrated time and time again.

Silvia took Claudia to the little cafe in the swimming pool complex and they waited for the others there. By the time the other mothers and babies arrived Claudia was happily drinking hot chocolate from "a big cup" and was looking proud of her achievement. Silvia didn't refer to Claudia's "failure" to get into the water and fortunately no-one else did either. Thus Claudia was allowed to go home with a sense of achievement, able to tell her dad that she had "hot chocolate from a *big* cup". Silvia "contained" her daughter's fears and anxieties; she did not make Claudia feel she had failed her but was able instead to give her the experience of success.

On the next visit Claudia still refused to go right into the water, but accepted sitting at the shallow end, on the steps, between her mother's legs. On the third occasion she made it into the water without anybody making a big thing of it. Over the next few months Claudia began to enjoy more and more the group's visits to the swimming pool and the casual observer would never have guessed the unpromising start to this. Silvia had made it possible for Claudia to enjoy the swimming pool.

At three and a half, when Claudia started nursery school, she settled in quickly. Her mother's patience and faith in her daughter had paid off.

Respect and the development of trust

Part of bringing up a child is the expectation that they will learn to respect others, and failure to do so is frequently punished. But children first need the experience of being respected themselves, then they can develop self-respect, from which respect for others follows.

Allowing the child to be himself or herself is in reality very hard to do. It takes trust in our capacities to be good parents. We want the children we have produced to be good, to demonstrate our own worth, and often to fulfil hopes and ambitions we have not achieved for ourselves.

All of the time, from the minute the child wakes, we are vulnerable to being careless of the child's feelings and wishes. Knowing the child's feelings or wishes doesn't mean we will necessarily agree but it does mean the child is thought about and not dismissed.

Two year olds are not deaf (except of course where there is a real hearing loss) but many adults really seem to behave as if their two year old is. This is comparable to the "selective deafness" of the two year old who does not want to hear what you have to say. Adults sometimes talk about inappropriate subjects when their child is in the room, believing that, if they are not addressing the child, or "they are busy playing", the child will not hear. Nothing could be further from the truth, two year olds are learning, absorbing all the time and they hear everything. We cannot have it both ways, this is the way the two year old develops so rapidly.

Mrs Jackson, in moments of exasperation, and in the privacy of her own house, would exclaim "bugger!". Whilst visiting friends she accidentally knocked over her tea, at which her little two year old commented in a charmingly sympathetic but loud voice, "That *was* a bugger, wasn't it mummy." Why do two year olds always say most clearly the very words you wouldn't want them to?

At other times, what is only partly understood can cause enormous worries and anxieties for the child. Adults sometimes talk about birth, pregnancies, operations, death, separations, divorce and other problems all within earshot of the child. The adults' own urgent need to communicate and be heard outweighs respect, at that moment, for what their child can cope with. The child's consequent response, whether as bad behaviour or perhaps a bad dream later, seems mysterious to the parents, who are quite unaware of what they have inflicted on the child.

Elisabeth's family were having major rebuilding work done in their home. Things had gone badly wrong and an impasse reached where the builder refused to complete the work until paid and Elisabeth's parents refused to pay until the bad work had been put right. Elisabeth's mother, obviously very upset, was sharing this with sympathetic friends while their children played together. The other children played on, but Elisabeth became more and more distracted, hovering nearer and nearer to the group of adults. Elisabeth picked up the toy hammer from the tool kit and began vigorously bashing on the floor and then on various objects in the room (very much what her mum was saying she'd like to do to the builder). Unaware of any connection between her conversation and her daughter's actions, Elisabeth was roundly told off by her mother for being "a very naughty girl" and she collapsed into tears.

Many two year olds do not like too much hugging and kissing except from those close to them and even then they often like to initiate it. Of course a spontaneous hug or kiss from mum or dad, big brother or sister is usually received with pleasure. But, two year olds are often instructed to "kiss auntie goodbye", when it is only too clear that they don't want to. Why is he told to kiss auntie goodbye? Usually so that auntie's feelings are not hurt. This is an example of how we can expect the two year old to be more grown up than the adults. Sometimes the child may not want to kiss goodbye for reasons that are, if we are honest, only too obvious to us.

Janey's grandpa was affectionate with her but also a bit overwhelming. His way of playing with her was very physical, and his goodbyes were always the same – "give your old grandpa a big smackeroo!". Janey hated the big smacking noises grandpa made with his lips as he advanced on her. But one day she stood up for herself and said, "No, don't want to" and pushed at grandpa with her hand. Her mother told her off for being naughty and insisted she kiss grandpa like a good girl. Afterwards mum told her friend she'd felt terrible, Janey had been subdued all the way home in the car. She knew she had let her daughter down but was frightened to hurt her dad's feelings.

Similar situations arise for us all when, as parents, we are confronted with something our own parents do with our child which we find we don't agree with. We let our children and ourselves down when we revert to being the child needing parental approval, and unable to stand up against an idea or practice of our parents. If we can allow our children to challenge us, we may help them avoid this.

Anxiety about our children's behaviour leading to a wish to control them means we often put unrealistic pressures on our children before we have understood the situation.

Being naughty

By now, most two year olds will have heard the word "naughty!" from somewhere. Naughty often seems to mean, "I don't like what you did" or "you embarrassed me in front of other grown-ups". Or the parent may feel the child's behaviour was "intentional" in the same way as an adult's could be said to be.

Martin had never called his child naughty and did not believe in smacking. He was shocked when he saw his son playing with his soft toys and soundly admonishing them; they were called naughty, spoken to harshly, and several received a smack with the words, "You have been so naughty you'll have to have a smack!"

This sensitive father described how he had said to his son, "But we never smack you like that!", at which little David had blushed, looked confused and asked Daddy to read him a story. Martin had been left feeling even more guilty by what he felt to be his son's unwillingness to talk about it. He'd asked his wife, "Where did he get that from – is that how he really sees us, anyone hearing David would think we smacked him."

The two year old playing in this way is not showing what his parents are actually like but what the powerful parents of his imagination are like. Although of course some of the play draws on the behaviour, and particularly the verbal expressions, of the parents. The parents can hear echoes of their voice and expressions used. It is a pleasure to hear your child playing at being mum or dad when they are being loving, caring, nurturing – just how we like to see ourselves – but it can be a terrible shock and hurt to parental feelings to overhear a child roundly telling teddy, or a doll off, in a harsh voice that you feel convinced you've not used.

Bossy boots: the tyrant

Many parents find the bossiness of the two year old difficult to tolerate and all parents find it difficult to manage sometimes. This period of bossiness seems to be heralded by the discovery of that powerful little word *no* in the child's second year of life. By the time your child is two, he or she will have had plenty of experience in experimenting with the motive power of that small word and the big impact it has on adults.

The discovery of "no" is a very important and significant milestone on the road to independence. Even though as parents we often view the prospect of battles preceded by "No, I don't want to" and "No, I don't like it" with sinking heart, the child who hasn't really learnt the power of "no" and experimented with it fully hasn't yet discovered his or her sense of self. It is as important to be able to say "no" as it is to be told "no".

I think all parents hope their child will be able to stand

up for his or her self and to have a sense of self respect. Recent media coverage of child abuse has emphasised the child's need to know that they have a right to say no, and their sense of this begins in the family. It begins by being allowed the right to refuse and to question. If we don't treat our two year olds with this respect we cannot really expect them to feel that in certain selected situations they can say no.

Much of the difficult side of living with a two year old becomes easier if we understand why two year olds are bossy and what its developmental significance is. When two year olds are bossy it is often because they are worried or anxious about something.

Mothers and fathers are very powerful figures to the two year old. They are the most important people in his or her world. As parents we are very aware of the power of the child, to be helpful or obstructive, to make us feel good or bad about ourselves, and, in the ordinary, every-day sense to "allow us" to be on time or late for an appointment. In the midst of all this it is perhaps not so surprising how often as parents, we forget how we look to the two year old.

The two year old really believes that mum and dad know everything and can do everything and can understand everything. And they are so *big*. Try looking at the world from the two year old's height – it is a very different view of the world – one we have usually lost contact with. Tables are big, furniture is huge and adults, well adults, what does it feel like to reach the knees of those giants? When we try to imagine ourselves back into that position it can help us to think about discipline. Often if we can put ourselves in their shoes, see the world through their eyes, our anger evaporates and it all becomes much simpler. It becomes possible to see that our child is frightened or jealous or tired or provocative, and then there's the chance, seen from their perspective as well as our own, to find a way to respond that shows them we have understood. Often we find that the obstinacy then evaporates. When two year olds are being difficult by exerting power, it is a sign of increasing maturity and can be welcomed providing they haven't chosen too inconvenient a moment!

By this time, two year olds are discovering the power of speech and action, practice all the time and become increasingly adept at exercising choice. They can run away when you call, struggle when you went to put their coat on, or can demand, question and argue with increasing fluency. From two onwards the little child is moving from being a toddler into being a little boy or girl, and their personality begins to feel established. As your child becomes more competent horizons expand, *but* there is a price to pay for this – the two year old begins to realise how big the world is, how much he or she doesn't know and from the cheerful omnipotence of the one-year-old comes the shock, the impact of wider life experiences. The parents can do a lot to help their child to find exploring the world more exciting than it is daunting. It is hard to remember how much we take for granted what we have had to learn about. For example: the telephone. As adults we probably don't give a thought to this extraordinary machine, which makes it possible to talk to someone not in the room. Some adults understand this process technically, others don't, but sufficient experience of it tells them that it works, and that's enough. But what is the two year old to make of the telephone? Why does Mummy talk to it? Where does the voice come from? Where is the person she is talking to? He puts his ear to the phone – yes, he can hear Grandma's voice. Some two year olds laugh in pleasure, some look anxious and push the phone back to Mother.

Here is Alex who is fascinated by the phone. He knows it is important to his mother, he knows she sometimes talks to daddy or to Grandma or friends. Daddy telephones and Alex's familiar wail goes up. "I want to talk on the phone". His mother asks him to wait a moment but his voice goes on and on, "I want to talk – I want to talk". She hands over the phone and Alex says "hello" in a very adult voice but follows it instantly with "Bye", and thrusts the phone back into Mother's hands. Mother tries to continue, but Alex again demands the phone; the same thing happens. Fortunately his mother feels his anxiety and so can gently but firmly persist with her 'phone call, and then help Alex to understand why it was so hard for him to have a conversation.

Alex cannot manage a conversation with his father because he cannot see him. He longs to do it but can't. As adults in this situation, we have a reliable image of the other person, but the two year old relies on all his senses to keep an idea of "another". To have a disembodied voice coming through the telephone is part of what he knows of his father and yet is only a part. What's happened to the rest? This is more than the young two year old can manage and for the time being he turns away.

A few months later Alex can talk, briefly, to daddy on the phone, but soon drops it and rushes to get his painting which he pushes at the phone, shouting, "See daddy." Mummy starts to explain that daddy cannot see the painting. Alex gives her a bewildered look and climbs into his mother's lap, leaning against her chest. She says that she will tell daddy about his painting, which she does, and also tells Alex that he will be able to show daddy his painting when he comes home that evening. Alex accepts this quietly, but is subdued for a little while afterwards and seems preoccupied. At times like this it is very evident just how much learning and discovering there is to do about the world, and how much two year olds need help to tolerate the anxiety involved before they can want to know more.

At other times the child is not driven by anxiety but is

able to "play" with power and can enjoy a game in which he refuses to do something, perhaps chased by Mother or Father, called "a little pickle" and the game repeated over and over.

Unfortunately for parents, the two year olds' limited experience of the world means that their sense of timing is not always too good. Where is the mother who has not had the experience of getting everything organised to go out, needing perhaps to catch a bus or be somewhere at a particular time? She's remembered to leave plenty of time, but today is the day her son is *determined* to do his own coat up. He cannot be hurried – he really doesn't understand why he should – he has this huge task, called "doing up buttons"and usually mum is pleased when he tries to do things. Mum tries to "reason" with him but all her reasons are outside his experience. She becomes panicked, impatient, maybe exasperated. He feels bullied, confused and panicky. As he gets more panicky and feels threatened he digs his heels in harder.

There is no easy answer to this situation. Sometimes a mother may opt for insisting on taking a screaming, kicking, wriggling two year old off to the bus, or try to get him, in that state, into a car seat or push chair. Sometimes she will decide to let him do his buttons, if it is not really essential to leave that minute. It is worth reflecting that, in addition to the two year old's confusion and anger, it is no fun for the adult either to take off with a screaming child. It is exhausting and miserable for everyone.

Most of the time the two year old really isn't being unreasonable, but doing what he thinks you usually want him to do. Of course, two year olds, like everyone else, experiment and may choose the worst possible moment to find out what will happen when they say no, and sometimes they will be cross and want to provoke you. It is important for parents to try and sort out which of these situations, this one is. There is one crucial difference here though, and that is that the adults may be expected to have more reasoning power than their two year old child.

The child in the adult

There is nothing like having a two year old for bringing adults face to face with their own childishness. There can't be many parents of a two year old who under pressure have not become every bit as childish as the two year old has the right to be! A particularly vivid example of this occurred in a supermarket on a Friday night. The mother was pushing a shopping trolley with her little girl sitting in the seat. The little girl was about two and a half years old. Mother was preoccupied, checking her shopping list, and the little girl got bored and restless and tried to climb out. Mum put her firmly back, saying only "sit still", as she had no time for an explanation. The little girl looked puzzled, tried again, and this time her mother sounded crosser and with a raised voice said, "I told you to sit still". The child looked upset and sat quietly. Mother, flustered, dashed off to the end of the aisle to collect some things, probably thinking this would make things quicker. Her little daughter was sitting quietly now, so that at first Mother didn't notice that she had reached into the trolley, removed a packet of toilet rolls, and was patiently picking off the wrapping. Finally succeeding, she held the toilet roll aloft with a look of pleasure and success on her face, only to be met by Mother's horrified response, "Don't be so childish!" The little girl burst into tears and adults nearby stared, accusingly, at Mother. Poor little girl, but also poor mum. Shopping with a two year old can only be fun if there isn't much to buy, the shop isn't too busy and the child still feels that they have some of your attention. Perhaps being allowed to hold something or join in choosing the breakfast cereal. But we do not live in an ideal world and circumstances may force us into shopping at the worst possible time of the week and for the whole week's shopping!

Here the mother really had forgotten that her daughter was a child and exploring, just as she is supposed to do. Ordinarily this mother may have been delighted with her daughter's persistence, but under pressure and less in control, Mother herself is less adult, rather more like a two year old.

A balanced approach to bossy boots

What seems to be important is the effort parents make to be thoughtful, to reflect on what the child is doing rather than react. It isn't helpful to become a slave to the "tyrant" child – and it isn't helpful to be a bigger tyrant. You will always win – you know more about life. Some parents resort to smacking instead of thinking. But it's worth asking if you want your child to grow up fearful and compliant with no mind of his or her own, easily led without much capacity to stick at anything, or possibly a bully who has learnt that the only way to get what you want is to do what mummy and daddy do – find someone smaller and weaker and bully them.

If we want our children to grow up as imaginative, resourceful, flexible people, then we have an opportunity to help them, particularly during the "twos".

Discipline versus punishment

As parents, attitudes to discipline and punishment do not seem to depend entirely on social classes or ethnic or cultural groups. Much of our own attitude has been influenced by our own experience of being a child. The difficulty for most parents is in remembering what it felt like to be a child. It is much easier to react to what the child has done rather than to reflect on the meaning of it: to behave as if it is reasonable to expect from the two year old, the same as we would expect from ourselves. It is not the same for a two year old to hit their new baby brother or sister out of jealousy as it would be for an adult to do so. Of course the two year old needs to know you do not approve of such behaviour and that you must protect the baby, but not to be punished with all the outrage and anger that would be appropriate to the same action from an adult.

It is much easier to be a "thinking" parent if we have been a child who has been thought about, but many parents make a conscious and deliberate effort to do for their child some of the things their own parents were unable to do for them. Sometimes this might be the decision not to smack their child, as it was something they remembered as frightening and unhelpful. Other parents take the view that "it didn't do me any harm". This really means that as adults we cannot bear to face that our own parents were less than perfect. Being aware of our parents' imperfections as well as being aware of those qualities we love and admire them for, make it easier for us to be reflective parents, aware of our own imperfections. This allows us to allow our child to challenge us when we are unreasonable.

Regular smacking is different, it is a way of using adult strength to frighten and coerce a child into submission. The child cannot learn to understand from smacking *why* certain behaviour is required, only not to do it. It is only from understanding the *reason* for certain behaviour, and the reason not to behave in certain other ways – in order to protect others, their property and themselves, and out of respect for the feelings, needs and wishes of others – that self-discipline can grow. When, as adults, we smack a child, we have stopped thinking. Why not take time to explain why the two year old shouldn't do what he or she has just done? Perhaps sometimes because, if we were truthful, there is no good reason. Simply that their behaviour is embarrassing or inconvenient to us. Where behaviour does need checking, then thinking first, reasoning and explaining take much longer but are more rewarding.

Most parents have probably occasionally smacked their child, but few feel proud of it. Children who are not habituated to being smacked will be shocked by an unexpected slap and will probably realise that they have gone too far or that mum or dad had less patience than usual today and forgive.

Parents who smack their children routinely should not then be surprised when they always hit out when crossed or frustrated in any way. Some parents smack the child but expect the child to reason situations out. Children who hit out because they haven't had a model of questioning, reasoning and understanding, are going to have a hard time at nursery or playgroup, and later at school.

Some children who are smacked regularly become subdued and timid; they seem to expect to be hit and are vulnerable to bullying by other children and adults. Shouting and harsh measures such as withdrawing love and approval can have the same impact on a young child.

Going too far

Of course, two year olds can be very unreasonable in the face of parental reasonableness, and even downright provocative.

Curtis had been difficult from the moment he woke up that morning. All day long his mother had tried to keep her patience with him, understanding that much of his difficult behaviour was provoked every time she needed to do anything with the new baby. Late afternoon, when she was changing the baby's nappy, Curtis announced "I'm going to wee all over the carpet," and did so. His mother explained that she'd be with him soon, that she knew it was hard to wait, but this time her reasonableness seemed to have no impact. Curtis told her angrily, "I'm going to wee *again* all over this carpet." His mother recounted later how his look seemed to say "and there's nothing you can do about it''. Of course, this was true in a way; mum's arms were full of the baby. Here Curtis seemed unable to bear his helplessness to command his mother's attention as he used to and so he made his mum know at first hand what real helplessness felt like and how angry it made him feel. Unfortunately, at the end of a long day he was too effective. His mother shouted at him and then smacked him. She recalled how shocked she'd been at the volume of her voice and immediately wondered what the neighbours would think. It was the last thing she thought about as she went to sleep, she felt guilty smacking a little boy not much bigger than a baby. Curtis was immediately contrite, shocked by his mother's response; he knew he'd gone too far. Afterwards she talked to him about it. Curtis was "a little angel" for the following two weeks.

A child who is brought up to expect discipline rather than punishment develops some self-discipline in time, and therefore less of the parent-child contact needs to be conflict ridden. The child develops empathy and a conscience. The child who is disciplined learns to care some of the time when she or he has done something wrong; the child who is always punished is more likely just to try to avoid being caught. With discipline we help a child to discover the power of thinking things through and offer strategies for difficult situations. Punished behaviour may be suppressed but it remains unresolved.

The development of a conscience

Where parents manage to be respectful of their child most of the time and attempt to discipline rather than punish, then the two year old begins to develop a conscience. Your child feels guilty when he or she has done wrong and, rather than trying to hide misdemeanours, needs to draw them to parents' and other trusted grown-ups' attention.

Jack's dad returned home from work at bath-time. Jack

was crying and mummy explained that he'd stubbed his toe on the bath. Dad went to comfort Jack and said "Show me your toe." "No," said Jack, "I kicked Joe (baby brother) in the bath." Here he shows his guilty conscience; he has hurt Joe and doesn't therefore deserve dad's sympathy. In fact his conscience, like most two year olds, is harsher than his parents' would be. His wrong doing was on his mind and far from trying to conceal it, he blurted it out. Dad's response helped modify Jack's own harshness to himself but such harsh voices from the child's internal world continue to reveal their presence for some time to come.

A few weeks later this same little boy was visiting his much-loved grandma. When he arrived grandma asked Jack, "Have you done anything nice today?" "I kicked Joe right in the head," he told her. This was by far his worst misdemeanour so far and his parents had been visibly upset by it. Again, far from wishing to hide his "crime" Jack showed that it was uppermost on his mind: his parents' distress had given him food for thought and, far from being indifferent, Jack revealed that he cared very much, and was able to stay knowing that he had done wrong.

Louise's parents had very high expectations of her and believed in "stopping trouble before it started" by "coming down like a ton of bricks" on any bad behaviour. This resulted in them not giving her much room for manoeuvre; she was so often in the wrong. Louise had her friend Pearl to play, which had started off well enough but both children became tired. Louise wanted her favourite video on but her father said no because the grown-ups couldn't hear themselves speak. Louise asked two or three times more. Louise's mother told her she was naughty and if she asked once more she'd be sent to her room to be on her own. Louise looked frightened but she was also angry; she walked to the other end of the room and hit Pearl's mother, who looked taken aback but who said nothing. Then, checking that no-one was looking, she bent over and pulled Pearl's hair. Here we can see Louise having to resort to subterfuge; her parents, to her, are giants and therefore cannot be openly challenged, but her frustration and anger have to go somewhere. Far from the openness of Jack she is learning secrecy. Her parents' behaviour does not encourage reflection and the development of her conscience.

The development of empathy

As a conscience develops, so does empathy. Parents who have struggled to respond to their child reflectively will find that a child as young as two, has great capacity for feeling for others.

Jake was the youngest of three, with a gap of five years between him and his older brother. Jo, his mother, had particularly enjoyed Jake as she was far less anxious than she had been with the other two; the family's financial worries were over and she had given up work this time to be at home and just enjoy being a mum.

When Jake was two and a half, Jo's much loved father died unexpectedly. It was mid-morning when the phone call came and only Jake and Jo were at home. The shock was so great that Jo screamed "Oh no", before bursting into uncontrollable sobbing. She remembered afterwards that she "knew she shouldn't do this in front of Jake" but could not help herself. Jo tried to reassure Jake through her sobs but could not get any words out.

Jake got his blanket (the blanket he cuddled when he went to sleep at night) and put it into his mother's arms. He then climbed onto the couch and sat quietly next to her, gazing softly into her face. When her crying quietened, Jake stroked his mother's face and said "there, there", just as she did for him when he was upset.

Eventually Jo was able to explain the cause of her outburst. She told him simply and factually of the shock and how much she had loved grandad. Jake listened quietly to everything Jo said before climbing onto her lap and wrapping his arms round his mother's neck.

Jo marvelled at the experience, afterwards saying that Jake comforted her like an adult. She had felt very moved by his evident love and compassion and also felt fleetingly guilty at not being able to protect Jake from her upset, or to comfort him for his own loss. But most of all Jo wondered that her child, at only two, had so evidently taken in something powerful about what loving and caring is about.

We can't always protect our children from painful life events, we can only help them through as best we can. We would obviously prefer that the two year old doesn't have to confront the issue of death but what really seems to matter is that we have already given our child love and respect, and shown how difficult situations can be handled.

One of the mysteries of life is that we don't know the outcome of things which we would, given a choice, avoid. A child may grow stronger and more loving, as seems to have been the case with Jake.

CHAPTER TWO

YOUR 2 YEAR OLD AND THE FAMILY

The parents

For two year olds mother is still the centre of their world – she is the safe base from which the rest of the world can be explored. The mother is still essential as a guide in this process of exploration; she is needed to protect her child from experiences which cannot be managed and to ensure that a child's natural sense that the world is a magical place does not become dented. The refreshing way in which the two year old sees the world is one of the major pleasures for parents: Daniel, at two and three quarters, struggling to make sense of the conversation amongst his much older cousins about the nature of God and the fact that they understood God as being all around, responded by saying, "I wish God was a piece of chocolate, then I could eat Him and just have Him inside me."

As soon as something goes wrong or a child is ill or tired, the two year old immediately turns to mum. It can be very confusing and frustrating when there is constant fluctuation between dependence and independence. Jack, two and a half, always insisted that mum put him to bed, much as he loved his dad. Sometimes dad wanted to spend time with his son when he returned from work, whilst mum, at the end of a long day, would have been very glad of time to sit down. However, they realised that Jack felt pushed out by the birth of a little brother, Joe. Jack was very clingy and demanding for a few months, just when his parents would have welcomed seeing the more independent side of his growing personality.

Daniel, when two and half, had measles and ran a very high temperature. During the night, mum had taken him into the parents' bed next to her. The following day grandma visited and was commiserating with Daniel, saying "Poor boy, what a bad night you had." Daniel looked at her in confusion before he answered, "No! I slept in my mummy's bed." For Daniel, having had his wish to be next to mum during the night, far outweighed the misery of being ill.

There is often a fluctuation during this year in the preference for one parent over the other, sometimes an insistence that "daddy do it" or, on the other hand, "No, I want mummy." Except, of course, at those times when the child is tired, ill, hurt or frightened, when mummy will almost always be the one who is preferred and needed. This can be tiring for mothers, and hurtful for those fathers who might choose to be more involved. However, it is during this second year that very commonly, in most families, the importance of the father becomes much more observable.

The two year old does nothing by halves and tends to be passionate about both parents, where there are two parents in the family. At this age, too, a child shows a special interest in the parent of the opposite sex; little girls show openly flirtatious behaviour towards their fathers whilst little boys demonstrate their wish to show off their strength and be admired by their mothers. Passionate love for one parent can also be parallelled by intense rivalry with the other.

Daniel, when he was two and three quarters, came into his parents' bedroom still rather sleepy one Sunday morning. He seemed momentarily startled to see both parents together. With a very cross expression on his face he walked to his father's side of the bed and gave his dad a punch in the chest with all the two year old strength he could muster. Then, with a satisfied swagger, he walked around the bed to his mother's side, kissed her and climbed into bed next to her. This was so blatant that his father had trouble hiding his amusement. It is a narrow line that parents tread at times like this; to laugh or to react angrily can crush the two year old's growing sense of self, but equally, parents need to be careful not to encourage the illusion that the child could really replace the parent of the opposite sex. Two year olds can be very provocative and if the parent of the opposite sex joins in, and uses it to provoke jealousy in their partner, the two year old can quickly become confused and tyrannical.

Daniel both adored his dad and wished to supplant him. He told his mum that when he was older he would marry her; "What about daddy?" his mother asked him. Daniel thought carefully, a worried expression on his face, and then suddenly his face brightened, he had the answer: "daddy will be our little boy".

Here Daniel reveals that, in his love for daddy, he cannot bear his wish to take his place – it isn't as easy as that; his solution shows a delightful two year old logic – there will just be a change around; put Daniel in the desired place of daddy and daddy can have a taste of being a little boy!

Sophie, Daniel's friend, was passionate about her father and became a real daddy's girl. Everything she did was checked for daddy's approval; she snuggled up close to him at every opportunity, sometimes ordering her mummy to "go in the kitchen and get on with the cooking", the implication being that she should be left alone with daddy whilst mummy serviced them both! Soon she declared her intention to marry daddy and around this time was sometimes rough and spiteful to her mother when all three were together. When she was nearly three she was told that daddy couldn't marry her because he was married to mummy, and Sophie was his little girl. Sophie seemed depressed for a few days and then announced firmly, when the three were together, that when she "growed up" she was going to marry another man called – and here she gave the exact same name as her father's. This was said with great firmness as the final word on the subject. In this statement Sophie revealed both her acceptance and refusal to accept that life couldn't be just the way she wanted it.

This love for the parent of the opposite sex includes the wish for sensual contact, to stroke, hug and kiss. A little boy may have an erection, a little girl quite unconsciously wish to straddle her daddy's knees. This stroking and cuddling can quickly turn to aggression, and mummy or daddy may suddenly be hit. The frustration which Sophie revealed, of knowing that wishes are not facts, can reveal itself in these swift mood swings: the anger may then be swiftly followed by an over-loving solicitude towards the parent who has just been hit or a denial of the anger and attack. Sophie, when she had turned angrily on daddy, would shortly after kiss and ask, "Are you happy, daddy?", nodding as she asked her question. Her guilt at hurting daddy was too much for her and she therefore tried to deny that she had hurt him.

The passionate love the two year old feels is very touching and many parents can see in it the fore-runner of future loves. The two year old loves uncritically, wholeheartedly, just as the future lover will when falling in love for the first time.

Oliver at two and a half loved his mother with great passion; he often told her with great sincerity that she looked beautiful. One day, out shopping, mother tried on a dress. Both Oliver and Daniel were with her in the fitting room. As mother slipped the yellow dress over her head Oliver exclaimed, "Oh mummy, you look just like a princess, shall we play princes and princesses." "No she doesn't," said Daniel, puzzled, "she looks just like a yellow banana." By five Daniel had the more realistic view of his mother but also he was jealous of his brother's adoration of her!

The jealousy the two year old feels can make weekends hard. Just when parents anticipate a weekend together with pleasure, and mum anticipates with relief another adult around, the two year old can be more difficult than usual. Many mothers observe that their child is easier during the week when alone with them, and it feels puzzling that it can be harder work when there are two adults, until we recognise the force of jealousy. Like almost everything else we first learn about our own jealousy and its effects within the family. Sometimes the child's jealousy of the parents' relationship can be masked by jealousy of brothers and sisters.

The Single Parent Family

Today, more and more adults are bringing up children single-handedly. Most of these single parents are women. Sometimes an adult is left to bring a child up alone because of the death of a partner, but more commonly because the parents have divorced or separated. Sometimes a parent is a single parent by choice. Some parents, following separation, manage to remain a couple in the sense of being their child's parents. Where this can happen it is obviously better for the child. The ability of two year olds to differentiate what is real and what is phantasy is still not very strong or reliable, and thus small children can in phantasy feel responsible for the events around them. Thus it is not uncommon for them to feel that they have driven father or mother away. If the parents can remain friends and continue to share responsibility and love for him or her, the child will come to understand and believe that he or she is not the person responsible for the break-up of the parents' relationship.

Human nature being what it is, however, it is often the case that the divorcing parents' capacity to take an adult responsibility for caring for their child is diminished and the child can then become a pawn in the relationship. Two year olds are very vulnerable and need to be protected as much as possible from arguments they cannot understand but whose emotional impact they can certainly feel. It is a time when it is very important to remember that two year olds have ears.

Alice is two and a half; her parents have separated after a marriage full of rows. Their separation is recent and has been acrimonious. Alice is playing in her bedroom when the doorbell rings and her uncle arrives. Mother begins talking to her brother, complaining about her husband, when Alice chimes in from her room "That bastard!" Mother is shocked and tells Alice off, but then looks at her brother embarrassedly, realising that after all it is only what Alice has heard Mother herself say. Mother's own unhappiness and need to talk was so great she had forgotten that Alice could hear from her bedroom.

When Alice emerges from her room, at first she is bossy and aggressive with her much-loved uncle, telling him to "Go away", trying to pull him off the couch, and throwing her toy saucepans on the floor near to her uncle's feet, one at a time. Mother is puzzled and embarrassed by this hostility.

Later Alice asks her uncle to play with her, telling him that he is to be her husband. They start to play, "Go away" she tells him fiercely, but looking at him closely to see how he will respond. Uncle says, "If I'm your husband, then I must stay here." But Alice says, "I'll chase you away," and she chases him while he pretends to run away. She then says to him, "Now go to work," turns to her pots and pans and begins to "cook". She calls to her "husband", "Don't forget to come for your dinner." Dinner consists of leaves and grass from the garden which Uncle says he will pretend to eat. "No," says Alice, "really eat it!". Uncle repeats that he will pretend and he does a very good imitation of someone enjoying a delicious meal. Alice watches him thoughtfully throughout and seems to decide to settle for this. She continues to boss him about, however, as each time he says he's finished his dinner, she insists he eats some more.

Here we can see how much Alice's mind is full with her anxieties about "husbands and wives". Do wives drive their husbands away? Is she, Alice, powerful enough to do it? She seems to take on the role of her angry mother, shouting at the man to go away. But Alice also loves her father and her ambivalence is shown when she tells her uncle/husband to come back for his dinner. Her wish to nurture and feed is entangled with her wish to punish him and this is shown by her wish to make him swallow whatever she dishes him up. Perhaps like she herself feels; after all Alice has had no choice in what she sees and hears. She has had to "swallow" a lot of unsuitable stuff that hasn't done her any good, just as grass and leaves wouldn't do her uncle much good. Uncle's capacity to play good-humouredly, but without being bullied into doing what he knows is not good for him, seems to help Alice to work on a situation that is frightening and confusing for her. She can try the role of the powerful one and discover in her play that she isn't powerful enough to drive Uncle away or make him do what he doesn't want to do. Perhaps in time, with games such as this, she will come to trust that she didn't drive her daddy away.

Sometimes parents, unconsciously, "gang up" with a child of the same sex e.g. "girls together" against the men, or a woman will find it harder to love a son who reminds her of her ex-husband or partner with whom she is still angry. Knowing that this may happen can help us to guard against it and so protect our child.

Joan has a daughter of five and a little boy of two. Her husband has left her to live with another woman. Joan still loves her husband and is angry and confused. Most of the time she is able to love and care for both her children, but sometimes her unconscious anger against her little boy, Malcolm, or her identification with her daughter, Tracy, come to the surface. This is particularly so at meal times, when Tracy is always served first and ostentatiously given the biggest or choicest piece. Next Joan serves herself and then Malcolm, who never complains in spite of being the littlest one. Joan seems to see in Malcolm, his "greedy" father, for whom one woman is not enough, and in her daughter she seems to see herself, needing and deserving first consideration. Unconsciously she sets up a provocative arrangement which her daughter seems to soak up, taking for granted that she should have first choice and behaving very much like a spoilt little princess. Malcolm interestingly, although only two years nine months when his parents separated, seems more able than his sister to understand the situation. He adores his mother, who in the past has given her little boy much love and appreciation, and now uses past good experiences to help him weather this difficult time. When his mother makes comments, such as "just like a boy" or accuses Malcolm of being rough when in fact it is his sister who is the rough one, he does not seem to react aggressively, but is gentle and loving. At other moments, she can appreciate this, however there is a danger that Malcolm will get pressured into being the "little man of the family".

Here we can see how powerful the unconscious is and how parents are all vulnerable under certain pressures, to "act out feelings" that they are not consciously aware of. If they do so when they are tired or fed up how much more so are they vulnerable when there are real crises in their lives. Being aware of our vulnerability makes it possible to do something about our own needs so that they are not "taken out on the children".

Single parent by choice

More women are choosing to have a child when not in a permanent relationship. Adults raising a child on their own frequently make a very good job of it, they enjoy being a parent and by and large their child thrives. But it is harder work for a mother or father on their own and it is also harder work for the child. Usually there will be less financial support available, but the lack of emotional support is even harder.

Parenting a child is full of worries as well as pleasures. For example, measles, mumps, chicken pox may be commonplace but they are the source of enormous anxiety for all parents. You cannot but be anxious when a little child runs a fever, they are so small you wonder if they'll survive, even though you know thousands of children have had these childhood illnesses. It is very lonely to be alone, nursing a sick child. If you are one of a couple then there's always the chance that one of you is being brave, realistic and commonsensical, leaving the other to get on with the "worrying myself to bits", but if you are on your own you have no choice but to carry both – the real fear for the survival of your child, and common sense that says, of course he will survive, it is just a fever. When there are two of you, there's a possibility of taking turns to be up with the ill child and someone else to test one's fears on.

Even interrupted sleep and sleepless nights, things every parent has to put up with, are much harder for the single parent. There is no-one to let you have a lie in, no-one to recognise that you're exhausted. Some single parents deal with this by being omnipotent, behaving as if they can manage everything and that nothing fazes them. The danger is that the decision to bring a child up on one's own can make it harder to admit that being a single parent isn't easy. Fearing the criticism of two-parent families, or relatives who have a different model can also make the single parent defensive.

It seems important to recognise that the human being is a group animal, and dependence is part of our human nature. Single parents need to ensure that they too have other adults whom they can rely on and ask for the occasional favour. They can gravitate towards other single parents, and indeed much mutual support can be found here. But there is danger in the fact that all groups can only too easily turn into gangs. Or to put it another way – a group of people who ostensibly get together for companionship and support can end up even more isolated in this case from two-parent families. These groups will mostly be women together, and whilst women can indeed offer each other a lot, in order to develop a sense of self, boys and girls need role models of both sexes.

For the single parent, there's the risk of investing all the capacity for love and affection in the child, which can make exploring independence difficult. With two parents around the child can experiment; if cross with mum, then he or she can be with dad for a while. Also, mum and dad will have different strengths and weaknesses which give a child a wider range of models to observe and try out. Of course, one of the disadvantages of the two-parent family is that mum and dad can be played off against each other. In this situation, turning to dad if you're cross with mum, can be used against mum and thus becomes an emotional *weapon* rather than a *tool*. A range of tools at one's disposal, a range of ways of responding to any emotion or situation, has to be a good thing. Emotional weapons are another thing altogether.

A two year old who hasn't a father or mother will by this age have begun to notice the existence of dads and mums, and to make comparisons. If the single parent feels defensive about this then the child will feel that something is wrong.

Many single parents are taken by surprise by their child's noticing the "missing parent".

Sally is a little girl of two years three months, and the daughter of a mother who is a single parent by choice. Suddenly Sally began calling all men "daddy". The man in the greengrocers was her first choice, but it soon spread. This was embarrassing for Mother at first and she responded by saying, "Don't be silly, you know it's not daddy." Then she realised it wasn't that simple. Her daughter didn't "know" in the same way as her mother did that this man wasn't daddy. There had never been a father in Sally's life but she noticed that there were lots of daddies around. This mother realised that it was time to talk about daddies. She had reached 40 and felt her time for being a mother was fast vanishing. She therefore decided to have a baby even though she was not in an ongoing relationship. Clearly this is beyond a two year old's understanding. After discussion with friends she started by acknowledging to her little girl, "We don't have a daddy living with us" which was where her daughter had got to in her observations. Confirming the reality of what her daughter was then noticing allowed some of the child's anxiety to be contained. Mother also tried to answer subsequent questions simply but honestly.

Brothers and Sisters: Jealousy

Joanne is two and a quarter, her sister Jenny is five. Joanne admires her sister and wants to be able to do everything her sister can do. This has proved an enormous spur to her development, and Joanne can speak in complex sentences. The two sisters often play together and for periods of time it is quite amicable until a squabble breaks out, often provoked by Joanne's refusal to accept that *any* of the toys belong *just* to her big sister. When Jenny says, "This is my doll," Joanne adds, "And mine too." "No," says Jenny, "it's mine. Tell her mummy." When mummy tries to explain this to Joanne, Joanne still infuriatingly adds, "and mine too".

This is very frustrating for Jenny, who must feel that her determined little sister will take over everything, including Jenny's achievements. However, Jenny is well able to have her revenge! Jenny and Joanne played mummies and babies together, a favourite game. They each have a baby doll which they use as their own babies. As they play together they agree that the two babies are being fed. Joanne tells her baby, "Do a poo." Jenny says, "Put a nappy on her – you wear a nappy anyway." Joanne looks puzzled and pulls at the top of her trousers. She looks down into them and says, "Don't, see!". To which Jenny replies, "But you do at night." Joanne looks crushed – there is no answer to this. She pauses, her baby doll held dangling from one hand, her head on one side, and she looks far away, lost in thought. Suddenly Joanne's face brightens and she turns to her big sister, "Watch me run!". Joanne races across the living room, running very fast indeed, most impressive. But Jenny hasn't finished yet! "Watch me skip," says Jenny, and she does so very prettily, pointing her toes for extra effect. Not to be outdone by big sister, Joanne says, "Watch me skip." She manages only a little hopping movement. "That's not skipping," says Jenny with exaggerated patience. "You have to do it like this – one foot up, one foot down". Joanne stares down at her unobliging feet. She seems to realise that her feet can't do what big sister Jenny's can. Joanne puts her thumb in her mouth before suddenly racing off to find mummy.

Support

Brothers and sisters are also a source of companionship and support; together they can stand up against those first oppressors – the parents! When Daniel was nearly five, he was "caught" by his mother mixing up a concoction in the bathroom with his two year old brother. Mum was cross and began to tell Daniel off firmly, at which two year old Oliver put his arm around his big brother's shoulder and said to his mum fiercely, "Don't you tell my brother off!". In future life many brothers and sisters continue to be friends as well as a source of comfort.

The wider family

Families can be a blessing and/or a curse. Some parents' own families of origin live far away and therefore are not available as a source of support, advice and baby sitting, but also not as a source of interference and pressure.

If you are very lucky then you will have supportive parents, brothers and sisters near by. Children usually like to visit relations unless there is a very strained relationship. Most children who are fortunate enough to have them, adore their grandparents and in return are greatly loved and indulged. The grandparent relationship is a very important one, involving many of the pleasures of parenting, without the stress and responsibility. Many people have much more fun as grandparents than they did as parents – after all, grandchildren go home! At its best, the grandparent relationship offers a closeness but with less conflict than there can be with parents.

But grandparents, brothers and sisters can exert unhelpful pressures; be unduly critical and demand a conformity the child is not capable of, or may have ideas on child-rearing which do not match the parents. As always, the two year old is quick to pick up the atmosphere on these visits even when grown-ups are careful of what they say, and tension often quite unwittingly gets transferred to the child.

Sexual identity

For the two year old the world is a very mysterious place, full of wonder but also confusing. The two year old, therefore, seeks for rules in the universe, for things to be predictable and for this reason they can sound like little sexists.

Jake, when something needs mending, always insists, "daddy mend it", and gets cross at mum's suggestion that she can do it just as well as daddy. Mother's wish to bring her son up in a non-sexist way, is at odds with Jake's wish for clear differentiations to be made between the sexes. Jake also refers to the family car as "daddy's car", even though both his parents drive. He wants clear, firm categories so that he won't be taken by surprise. He has just had to accept that his mother can grow a baby inside and that he and his father cannot. He had spent some months before the birth of his baby brother insisting, "Got a beebee in here", pointing to his tummy. Similarly he asked everyone, young and old, male and female, "Got a beebee in there?" pointing at their tummies. At this point in time his possession of a penis and the role of the male in creating new life didn't impress him nearly as much as his own mother's changing shape, followed by her disappearance into hospital, the production of the baby, and then the feeding of him. Mother's changing shape had literally pushed him off her lap. In comparison, father's role seemed hard to fathom.

Joanne at two and a half hadn't questioned sexual differences, appearing to deny their existence; after all she and her big sister, Jenny, were made the same way. The fact that she had noted sexual differences revealed itself in an earnest conversation with a friend of her mother's who was visiting. "Have you got little girls too?" she asked. When she was told that her visitor had boys and her mother had interjected, "big boys", Joanne blurted out, "I have seen my daddy's bottom, and it is longer." Joanne's mother was taken aback as Joanne had never commented before. Joanne then added, "No, it is the same as mummy's because it's got fur around it," and then continued with her game.

Here, Joanne's wishes for clarity and her anxiety about sexual differences is revealed when she denies what she has observed because it leaves some unanswerable questions for her. Possibly the fear that she had "lost" her penis.

A new baby in the family

In many families there is a gap of about two years between the first and second or second and third child. Many parents feel that a two year gap allows the first child sufficient time to be the baby and to begin the move towards independence, whilst having the advantage that, as time goes on, the children can become friends and companions to each other.

Preparing for a new baby

Forty years ago few children were prepared for the birth of a brother or sister; myths abounded and children were told that babies were left by the stork, brought by the doctor, found under a mulberry bush, and so on. Fortunately nowadays most parents realise that children have ears and eyes and none more so than the two year old. It is inconceivable that a two year old could miss his mother's changing shape; her preoccupation at times with her pregnancy, especially if she feels unwell with it, as well as overhearing her conversations with other adults.

It is difficult to know how much to tell the two year old and when. Most parents feel they want to wait two or three months to feel reasonably confident that the pregnancy is securely established. Because two year olds are so sensitively attuned to their mothers, and because they listen so hard to everything that is said, it can be hard to delay talking to the child until the three months has passed. When children "pick something up", rather than being told, then all sorts of distortions creep in.

Most children are helped by being told simply that mummy and daddy are going to have another baby and that the baby is growing in a special place inside mummy. This information will usually then be followed by the child's own questions. There may be a delay between being given the first piece of information and the questions that follow. But in this way the information you supply is guided by what the child wants to know.

Sometimes parents are so worried that the news will upset their two year old that they force more facts than the child is ready for. They may also give false reassurances and untruthful statements, such as pretending that mum is pregnant solely to provide a friend and playmate for the two year old. This cannot succeed, since the child may well tell you, as Claudia told her mum, "I've got friends already" or, when the baby is born, the discovery will soon follow that the new baby brother or sister isn't any good to play with, and the child will therefore feel betrayed. It also helps to say that the baby will not be born for a long, long time. Even then, you may well be asked over and over, "Is the baby coming today?".

The facts of life

Here again it helps to be guided by what your child asks you. Providing you make it clear that you are happy to answer all questions, then over the months, as the questions occur, your two year old will ask them.

However, you need to be prepared for the fact that even when the facts have been given, the child will continue to hold his or her phantasies as to how the baby got in, and how it will come out, and what it's like in there for the baby.

Daniel, seeing his very pregnant mother in the bath, pointed to her tummy and asked worriedly, "Can the baby breathe in there, under water, or will it drown?". Later, when Oliver was born, Daniel talked of the time he was inside mummy's tummy, together with his brother and his mum and dad. Daniel somewhere knew that this wasn't the case but it was also a reality for him – his family, at two and a half, was still his world and he was unable to imagine that life before birth could be any different from life after.

Some children, such as Jake, insist that they too have a baby in their tummy and around this time, the child who seemed to be happy to use the potty or toilet may suddenly become reluctant to do so.

Arrival of a new baby

Most parents are prepared for the two year old to experience and show some jealousy, but it can still be a surprise to discover, how, even when prepared for a new baby's arrival, the two year old shows us that for him it is a shock; his or her nose is really out of joint. Nothing can fully prepare such a young child for the reality. Mummy is tired and new babies need so much feeding, cleaning and cuddling – inevitably there is less attention for the two year old. Many small children have asked "When is the baby going back?" after a few days or weeks. It is wise not to expect the child to be too helpful, rather the opposite. Many mothers share the experience that just as the baby has settled to feed, the two year old chooses to urgently need a "wee", or to get into some difficulty that involves mum in putting the baby down to attend to him or her. The two year old's mixed feelings may also show in the way the baby is hugged too hard, or toys thrown towards the baby. At other times genuine affection is shown by stroking the baby or bringing things for the baby to play with or fetching mummy when baby cries.

Jealousy and resentment are natural responses in this situation, and an open display of feelings is a healthy indication of the child's trust in their parents and in their sense of themselves.

Some parents become very worried by their child's jealousy, perhaps because they have never really learned to manage their own, and emphasise the importance of the two year old at the expense of the baby. One couple described how they put the baby in front of the TV for hours on end to keep her quiet so as to continue to give the same attention as before to their two year old daughter.

This obviously isn't very helpful; the baby is not getting the attention needed and this, at some level, may make the older child feel too powerful and lead to tyrannical behaviour and guilt. Sooner or later we all need to learn about, and manage, our jealousy. If we learn to share our parents' attention, first with siblings, then later we will be able to do so in our friendships and with a future partner.

Managing the needs of a two year old and a new baby needs patience, imagination and resourcefulness on the part of parents. The two year old is little more than a baby him or herself, but is learning new skills all the time. It is a delicate balance to help the child towards maturity whilst allowing for ongoing, and appropriate dependence. Inevitably we will often get it wrong and find ourselves on the wrong side of the line.

Sometimes the two year old copes with this difficult time by taking on the character of someone admired from a book or TV programme, as you will see with Jack, later in the book, when he becomes Fireman Sam, sometimes by "playing" at being baby and wanting you to pretend too, or by taking the baby over and becoming "mummy". Often the two year old will revert to behaviour previously outgrown, such as disturbed sleep, wetting during the day, constipation, or sudden fears and phobias, or a new faddiness with food.

Toilet training versus readiness to be clean and dry

Most families start to think about their child beginning to use the potty from 18 months on. There used to be a great emphasis on training even small babies but nowadays most people agree that it makes sense to wait until your child is ready; that is, until she or he is able to control the sphincter muscles.

Children vary enormously in their readiness to be clean and dry during the day; some seem to learn within a week; most become reliable over a few months from starting to learn. But the two year old can still have "accidents" or may suddenly become unreliable again. The birth of a new baby often puts the two year old back to wetting just when it would be particularly helpful to the parents not to have two "babies" needing cleaning up.

If your two year old isn't yet able to judge when he or she needs the potty, it seems to be an area of development where a relaxed attitude is particularly helpful. Many a child who didn't seem to have a clue at 18 months learns easily at two and a half.

The whole issue of having your child clean and dry includes a lot more, of course, than the child's capacity to control the sphincter muscles. Most adults have strong feelings about excretory functions, and are uncomfortable with references to their own. Some adults find the business of changing nappies disgusting, and therefore cannot wait to have the child clean and dry.

The child's attitude to urine and faeces

Many young children want to play with their stools and urine and are fascinated by this stuff which their body produces. As parents we often give mixed messages. We are interested in whether or not our child needs a wee or poo, whether, after sitting on the pot or toilet, they have actually done a poo, saying "good boy" or "good girl" and being very pleased with these products. But then things change. Mum or dad now wants to dispose quickly of these "treasures" whilst the two year old can want to hang on to them. It is all a matter of intense interest and fascination for them, and a subject for open discussion. Daniel greeted a male visitor emerging from the toilet, with "Did you have a nice poo?", said in his most charming, sociable voice.

The child's phantasies

As adults we take for granted that we know what urine and faeces are: body waste for disposal, associated with germs, bad smells, and embarrassment. The two year old, for a time, is more aware that it is his or her creation which, if given to parents in the right place, will please them. The child's readiness to use the pot or toilet coincides with growing independence and sense of self and with it a wish to give pleasure as well as the power to withhold it. After all, it does feel as if we have been given a real present when our child chooses to "perform" in the right place. No more nappies.

There is for the child some sorting out still to do: are the faeces and urine really a part of his or her body? Is it really so different from other "parts" of the body. Whilst this clarification is going on many children are reluctant to allow parents to dispose of the contents of the pot. Some compromise usually helps here: Daniel was happy to have the contents of the pot emptied into the toilet provided the toilet wasn't immediately flushed. Later Daniel would allow mum, without distress, to flush the toilet, providing he could first wave his "poos" goodbye. Many young children do not like using the toilet outside their own family home, and indeed many adults have a preference for their own toilet.

The loud flushing of the toilet may stir a child's fear of being flushed away with the part of themselves they've only just relinquished. Usually these preoccupations are short-lived.

Phantasies around mother's pregnancy

Jack, soon after his brother was born, had a minor illness during which he became constipated. Passing his stool was very painful and he became very fearful of using the toilet at all. The family G.P. gave some medicine to soften the stool but this didn't seem to help. Jack seemed determined to "hold on to his poo". He'd previously learnt to use the pot and then the toilet quite easily, now all seemed to be lost. He was obviously in great discomfort and, as his mother put it, "bursting to go", but he wouldn't give in. Jack also began to object to the smell of his faeces. Gradually he revealed that the birth of his brother from inside his mother's tummy had got him thinking about what was in his tummy and what he produced. Earlier in mother's pregnancy he had insisted that he had a baby in his tummy and now in his very constipated state his distended tummy made him indeed look pregnant. Unconsciously Jack tried to deal with his resentment about his mother's pregnancy, by having his own; the trouble was, he couldn't produce babies, just "smelly poos". Careful talking and listening gradually resolved the situation but for some time he retained a great sensitivity about the smelliness of his faeces.

Feeding and feeding fads

Some children never give cause for concern where eating is concerned. As babies they suck well, are never sick or colicky, move on to solids with pleasure and continue to eat, with a healthy appetite, a good range of food. But growing up is rarely that simple for most of us. The feeding relationship is intimately linked to the relationship to mother, right from birth. There is no more effective way to show anger or resentment with mother than by refusing her food, and probably most parents have a tendency to over-react when their child seems off his or her food, just because the feeding situation is so emotionally loaded. Many children go off their food or become picky when a new brother or sister arrives, or at any time that is emotionally exhausting and for which, of course, the two year old holds mother responsible, as always. Thus a move of house, or illness, or even a holiday can stir anger, resentment or confusion, which reveals itself in the child's attitude to food.

The development of feeding fads can be aggravated by adults' attitude to food. Are meal times calm, peaceful and enjoyable? Is food something to be savoured? When your child first moved on to solids was he or she allowed to 'play' with their food? If we expect too much from the two year old the meal times can easily become a misery. It's not realistic to expect a two year old to sit quietly through a long family meal. To be allowed a toy between courses or perhaps to leave the table and return, eases the situation for everyone.

It's helpful to make your attitude to food as relaxed as possible and not to be unduly worried if your child temporarily goes off his or her food Coaxing, "just eat one more mouthful" makes the child too powerful and too anxious, a disastrous combination; having an anxious parent hovering over a child confirms the child's fear that there really is something to be worried about.

Fears and phobias

Two is the age at which parents may first see fears in their child that they cannot understand. Many two year olds become afraid: of the dark, of dogs, of particular people, of a piece of clothing. These fears are related to the child's imaginative life. Two year olds are often frightened by the power and intensity of their own feelings but without enough life experience yet to be sure that they will not actually succeed in destroying whoever they feel murderously angry with. Sometimes it's possible to trace the appearance of a frightening monster to a ferocious outburst earlier in the day.

Other fears are connected with the child's incomplete understanding, for example, of sexual differences. Stephen became very anxious about using the toilet and began insisting that his mum check the window was closed before he could agree to do so. His mum went along with this and wisely did not tease him or call him silly, although she hadn't any idea why he needed the window closed. One day he added the information, "Close the window in case a bird comes in." Still puzzled, his mum asked "What would the bird do?" "Peck off my willy," was the reply. Stephen had recently become aware that little girls were made differently, supposed they had lost their willies and he was just making sure he didn't lose his too.

CHAPTER THREE

YOUR SOCIABLE 2 YEAR OLD

The importance of play

Often as adults we give little thought to the importance of play for the child, but the two year old begins to play from the moment they wake up. When children play they are also working, and their absorption and concentration sometimes reveal just how *hard* they are working.

Whilst two year olds play, they are working out the difference between imagination and reality; working out the way people and things in the world behave; trying on different roles and practicing skills. Children also play in order to cope with powerful emotions, such as love and hate, often by ascribing these feelings to a favoured teddy or doll.

At this time wishes and deeds are often confused. Tracy, two and a half, was playing mummies and babies. She took her baby doll and began to undress it. She looked at her baby doll's bottom and checked to see if she had done a poo. Tracy peered closely at the baby doll's bottom, frowned, and then turned to her mummy and said, "Just 'tend." This seemed also to reassure

Tracy herself. For the two year old the gap between imagination and reality is not always clear and for a second or two Tracy "forgot" that she was playing and expected to find a real poo. Magical thinking persists for the two year old and indeed some magical thinking continues into adult lives, as is revealed in superstitions, good luck charms and mascots.

But, most importantly, play is pleasure. It is fun; in play the child learns creative ways of overcoming the obstacles life sets before him or her and the capacity to play has a profound effect on future development. If as children we have the opportunity to play in all kinds of ways and are encouraged in this by parents, then we have the foundations securely inside us for continuing to meet obstacles creatively in the future, and even to enjoy a challenge.

Toys

Children do not need expensive toys – they often choose to play with household objects; most two year olds prefer real saucepans and wooden spoons to toy ones, and improvisation by imaginative and playful parents is a good model for the child. Some children reassure their parents early on of their capacity to improvise toys. Sam at two and a half was found sitting on the bottom stair with three pebbles he had brought in from the garden. He was playing an involved and imaginative game of mum and dad with their little boy (he had left his big brother out of this game!). He played this game for three quarters of an hour entirely to his own satisfaction and when it was time for bed the three pebbles were placed beside him on his bedside table and talked to most affectionately and wished goodnight.

Educational toys have their place but it is important also to have toys which help the child sort out the real and imaginary world.

Some parents worry endlessly over what toys to provide

and whether or not to provide certain toys at all. Parents seem less anxious than they used to be that if they give a boy a doll he will turn out to be effeminate, or that by giving a girl a garage she will turn out unfeminine. When parents are flexible and not anxious, then their children will have the opportunity to explore different aspects of themselves in their play.

Many parents worry about violence and hope to circumvent it by not allowing toy guns or swords. One father described how all toy weapons had been forbidden in his house, only to find his son and daughter racing around, shooting each other with "guns" made from Lego. In playing, children discover something about their own aggression.

Daniel's parents allowed him toy weapons. Some years later he saw news coverage of war on television. He watched in evident distress and then said, "Those soldiers are children's daddies and women's husbands and" – after a pause – "they have mummies too. I don't like war, I wouldn't want to kill anyone." He sank into a thoughtful silence and then said, "I wouldn't like to kill anyone but I do like playing with guns, but that's not the same, is it?".

Creativity

Sometimes as adults we have an idea of how something should be done and may not take time to notice that our child has something else in mind. Two year olds need plenty of encouragement and not too much criticism, as they are only too aware of their smallness and incompetence. In play they have the chance to discover their own creativity.

Matthew is two and a half and has just come home from his all-day nursery to be with his mother and father. Matthew wants dad to play horsey with him but dad is tired and refuses to play with Matthew. He suggests to Matthew that he build another tower like the beautiful one he had made yesterday.

Matthew beams broadly and quickly fetches his box of building cubes. As he picks up each cube he asks himself, "Is this big? Is this small?". It is a mixture of question and answer. Matthew uses up all the cubes and when this tower is finished he knocks it down, saying in a saucy way to his dad, "It fell down." His dad smiles and Matthew then begins again. He is engrossed now and seems, too, to be experimenting – each cube is examined closely and from several angles. This time the tower is different; he has balanced big on small alternately, and it clearly takes considerable skill to achieve this. Mother now notices and says to her son, "No, that's not right" and patiently begins to explain again how he should start with the biggest and so on. Matthew looks miserable; he is unable to explain to his mother what he had in mind and clearly just feels that he has failed. He knocks his tower down again, but this time full of anger and despair.

Play to master jealousy

Jack is two and a half and has a baby brother of a few months old. Jack is still recovering from the shock of this new baby's arrival and is often cross and difficult. Jack loves the TV programme for children called "Fireman Sam". Fireman Sam is a helper; he gets people out of difficulties whilst other characters in the story are both naughty and silly. Jack had been given a Fireman Sam's helmet as a present and from that moment on he wore it all day long, and even wanted to sleep in it at night. The minute he woke up, on it went. He even insisted on wearing it in the bath!. One morning, when mum went in to get Jack, she kissed him and called him Jack but he answered very firmly, "I'm not Jack, I'm Fireman Sam." In his imagination, the house had become the setting of the fire-station and of the fireman Sam stories.

As they go out for a walk that day, Fireman Sam/Jack

drives his pretend fire engine. He rescues people and tells naughty people off. His baby brother is given the role of a naughty character and his mother of another character. For three weeks he answers only to the name "Fireman Sam". He also insists on watching a Fireman Sam video over and over again. Here we can see Jack dealing with his misery and jealousy, and frequent extreme unhelpfulness in the face of the birth of his baby brother by becoming an extremely helpful fireman and letting others be the naughty, silly ones. In this way Jack manages creatively to get through the most difficult period after his baby brother's birth. Three weeks after he woke demanding he be referred to as "Fireman Sam", he reverted to answering to Jack, although still loving Fireman Sam and his helmet. It was noticeable that from this point on, he became able to have a more balanced and friendly relationship with his baby brother.

Play to master separation

Jake missed his dad very much during the working week. Sometimes dad left before Jake was awake and returned when Jake was asleep, but they enjoyed the weekends together. Jake often played "going to work", announcing, with a very important expression, that he's off to work and that mummy and his baby sister should wave goodbye. He would empty his toy doctor's case, and emulating father's mysterious briefcase, pack it full of things which "mummy and his sister mustn't see". Jake hasn't really yet got any idea of what dad does when he's gone all day.

The day dad returned to work after the Christmas holiday, Jake insisted on playing the game over and over again. He wanted the real front door opened, to stay outside for a minute and then be welcomed home. This was not very easy to go along with on a cold, January day. All imaginative substitutes suggested by his mother such as using the hall as the pretend outside, were adamantly refused on this occasion. Play here was used as a way of managing a situation which Jake was finding hard to bear. He tried to cope with his father's disappearance by "being dad" and making mummy and his sister the ones who were left behind. Because he was upset at losing dad after the holiday he was not able to use suggestions from his mother and could not imaginatively substitute the hall for the outside. His play was an attempt to deal with overwhelming feelings in the face of not really having a proper understanding of why his dad had to go to work at all.

The next weekend dad found a very grumpy Jake. This was very hard for his dad to take, as he had been looking forward to spending the weekend with his little son. Fortunately mother, who had been watching Jake play this game over and over all week, was able to share her understanding of it with her husband, that Jake was actually very upset and did not understand why dad had to go to work. He thinks that he could have stayed at home and played with him if he had wanted to. This understanding made it easier for dad to put up with his son's grumpiness. Dad's resilience in the face of his bad temper seemed to reassure Jake that his father did indeed love him very much, and led on to lots of questions about going to work, which his father did his best to answer.

Imagination and reality

Josy and her sister, Pam, who is six, have invited Sarah and Nicola to play. For a while all four play together and then the two older girls, Pam and Nicola, go off to the end of the garden, telling the younger ones they can't come, they're not big enough.

Josy looks troubled, and stands for a while with her thumb in her mouth staring after her big sister. She then begins a game with Sarah – an imaginative game in which they prepare food for a restaurant. Josy suggests pizza and they discuss toppings, most of these orthodox – cheese and salami, but also some flowers, and some stones. When they have been prepared they are put into a pretend oven. Josy then says, "But they can't have any can they," indicating her sister and Nicola. "No," agrees Sarah, solemnly, "'cos they're naughty, aren't they?" adds Josy as she nods in agreement with her own words. Josy then picks up the first of the pizzas and hurls it onto the grass in the direction of the big girls. Sarah follows suit with the second. They both laugh but then Josy turns guiltily to check if mummy has seen through the window.

Here Josy is trying to deal with her hurt and anger when her big sister seems to need to emphasise Josy's littleness.

Josy first explores her own creativity, which she does with the cooking play, then wants to exclude Pam as *she* has been excluded (Pam is to be given none of this delicious pizza), and finally she vents her anger and frustration, by hurling the pizza in Pam's direction.

Pam is too big and powerful in relation to Josy, to be tackled head on but in her play Josy has the opportunity to work through these difficult feelings, which she does most effectively. However, fantasy and reality are still not clearly differentiated as she shows both in the play with the pizza where leaves and stones can go on pizzas as readily as real food and when she turns guiltily after hurling the plate. Her wish to hurt Pam as she had felt hurt was strong and at two and a half she cannot distinguish her wish to hurt Pam from guilty fear that she has really succeeded.

Phantasy and dreams

Phantasy is used to describe those ideas, thoughts and feelings we all have around any incident but which may not be readily known to us. Phantasies are more than the daydreams or ideas and feelings we are aware of. Much of our phantasy life is unconscious and as adults we may be most aware of this because of our dreams.

Phantasies carry on into the night time as dreams and nightmares. It is around two that many children first become aware that they have had a dream. This is an enormous developmental step since it indicates that the child is developing an awareness of different states of mind; of being awake and being asleep. When a child first wakes, particularly from a nightmare, he or she may feel that the nightmare was a "real" event. Something that we can still experience during our adult lives. When a child can talk of "having a dream" we know that they can distinguish "real" and "imagination".

Daniel, waking from a nightmare when just two, could only stammer, "'Umpty Dumpty, 'Umpty Dumpty", and sob in great distress. Gradually the picture emerged that he had dreamt of Humpty Dumpty falling off the wall and being all in pieces.

Stephen suddenly remembered a dream when eating breakfast. He turned brightly to mum and said, "I had a dream in the night." He then recounted this dream, pausing to say half way through, "and then there were the adverts", and he then told the second half of his dream. His mother was very much amused to hear that his nice dream, just like his favourite TV programme, had interruptions for advertisements.

Problems with sleep

There are often patches when the two year old child has trouble sleeping; either with going to sleep or with waking during the night. These new disturbances in sleep are usually short-lived. Sometimes an external cause is obvious to the parents; the arrival of a new baby, starting nursery school, an illness, sleeping away from home on a holiday, can provoke a disturbance in sleep. Sometimes the cause is less obvious, but when we begin to reflect on all the developmental changes that have occurred during such a short time, perhaps it will be less surprising. Moving out of the safety of the family into the wider world, the two year old has to match himself or herself against other children; manage without mummy and daddy for a time when with friends or at nursery school or playgroup. The world is more exciting but less safe. Sometimes a child over-reaches himself or herself and sometimes parents have expected too much. By the time bed-time comes, a two year old may have too much on his mind, just as can happen to us as adults, and may feel tense because it hasn't been possible to play things through satisfactorily during the day. The child is also more aware of jealousy, as already described, and bedtime means 'letting go', allowing mum and dad to be alone, or an older brother or sister to be up when they have to be in bed. This can stir anger and resentment, but also sadness. A temper tantrum before bed can also disturb sleep.

Tracy had been very angry with her mum, who suspected that things hadn't gone well at playgroup. Just before bed Tracy had an explosive temper tantrum, during which she hit mum. Her mother had managed not to lose her temper, but during the night Tracy woke very distressed, mum went in to comfort Tracy, but to her shock and distress, Tracy shielded her face as her mother approached her cot and shouted "Go away, go away", making mother feel like a monster. Only dad could comfort Tracy, and Tracy continued to look frightened when mum tried to approach her. Tracy seemed fine in the morning but it took her mother some time to recover.

Here we can see the origins of the witch in fairy stories. Tracy behaved as if mum would hurt her, and probably had been dreaming of a witch-mum. Clearly this was not due to mum's behaviour – she'd not lost her temper with Tracy. But Tracy had hit mum and had a harsh conscience inside her, harsher by far than the treatment she'd received from her parents.

Anxieties such as these can make a child frightened to go to sleep or to need to have a light on. It is the two year old who "discovers" monsters, witches, things under the bed and strange noises at night, as unresolved events and emotions of the day come back in concrete form. Usually a calm, patient response works and mum and dad are helped in this by their own memories of being frightened as a child.

Of course the two year old can "try it on" at bedtime, with endless requests for another story, another drink, and needing another "wee". This requires patience but also kind firmness, which re-assures the child that his or her fears are groundless, whereas calling the fear silly does not. Endless checking of the child or "pandering" to requests only serve to feed the anxiety that something is wrong.

Communication: Language

The year between two and three is particularly exciting, as the child's capacity to communicate and to understand the communications of others increases so dramatically. Speech increases all the time and your two year old can understand everything you say. Parents and children can have proper conversations in which the child reveals so delightfully their perspective of the world. Daniel had been read a young child's picture book version of Gulliver's Travels. Later when out with his parents he saw a tall chimney on a factory and exclaimed, "That's a Gulliver of a chimney!". At the beginning of the second year it may be only the parents who can understand their child's speech but, as the year goes on, it usually becomes possible for people outside the family, children and adults, to understand as well. This opens the world up for the child. Needs can be made known more easily and visits to friends and playgroups made more readily.

Children acquire language at different rates. Some two year olds speak fluently and in sentences early on, others when they are nearly three. There is only cause for concern if a child approaching three seems uninterested in speech; or perhaps earlier if a child does not seem interested in communicating and being with people at all, especially if this extends to their parents.

Parents can do a great deal to encourage the development of language and to make communication fun. It is enjoyable to take the trouble to describe situations to the two year old; to explain how things work and to prepare them for the events of the day. Sometimes parents get into a habit of using speech mostly to correct or nag at the child, and this is unlikely to encourage anyone to want to talk. It was noticeable that Timmy's speech was slow in coming and his mum worried about this with her friends who had children of a similar age. She seemed unaware, however, how much she used speech to express negative feelings about him. Her voice often had a weary note as she told him constantly not to do this or that; and a weary "Oh, trust you, Timmy" greeted what mum saw as his constant failure. Speech for Timmy had become connected with disappointment and failure.

When the two year old begins to discover the power of language, that it is a key to the mysteries of the universe, then we start to hear "Why?", only to find that the answer to that question is swiftly followed by another, which can also become exhausting for parents!

In the following example we can see Tom struggling to understand one of the mysteries of the world – why grown-ups can do some things which two year olds cannot.

Questioning and understanding

Tom is playing at Jack's house and is fascinated by the music centre in the corner which houses the record player, radio and tape machine. It seems like a magnet to him and he cannot stay away from it. His mother tries repeatedly to deflect him gently but Tom becomes more and more insistent. He keeps asking why he can't touch it and his mother's thoughtful and reasonable replies don't satisfy him. Finally she resorts to that age-old, "somebody else's responsibility", reply saying "It belongs to Jack's dad and he won't let anyone touch it." Tom becomes thoughtful at this. Tom has a sister, Daisy, two years older than himself and a brother, Mark, two years older than her. He asks his mother, "Would Jack's dad let Daisy touch it?" His mother says "Oh no, Daisy wouldn't be allowed to touch it either." "Well then, would Mark be allowed to touch it?". "No," his mother tells him, "Mark wouldn't be allowed to touch it either." Again Tom is thoughtful. "When I'm as big as Mark, can I touch it then?", his fingers drawn again to the tape machine, only to be gently removed. "No," said his mother, "you won't be able to, but you could have a little record player of your own when you are a bit bigger." She indicates a toy one which his friend has in his living room. Tom is quickly dismissive, "I don't want a toy one, I want one with all the buttons on to press." His mother explains that he is not old enough to have one of those. Tom holds his hand above his head and says, "When I'm as big as this can I have one then?". She says "No, you still won't be ready." He cannot leave the topic alone. He comes back to it again and again. Finally he says, "Well, when I'm a daddy can I have one then?" and his mother agrees that when he's a daddy he will be allowed to have one. At first he seems satisfied by this and goes off and sits on the floor and begins to play. However he drops the toy which he'd returned to, and sits, slumped forward slightly, his head dropped on his chest. Suddenly he turns towards his mother and says in a very cross, reproachful voice, "I'm only a little boy you know."

As usual, with children of this age, mother is held responsible for everything. Tom puts his complaint to his mother that he's only a little boy, which seems to mean here something like "You really can't expect me to do all this sorting out you know." Fortunately his mother smiles at him and says only, "I know you are, Tom," and he is able to play after this.

The increased capacity to reason

With increased competence to use language, so comes an increased capacity to reason. Elisabeth, in the following example, uses language to question and explore ideas with others but we can also see her 'thinking', that is, having a conversation inside her own head.

Elisabeth, at two years 10 months, is a competent and verbal little girl. She is visiting her friend, Jack, and his baby brother, Joe. She has been playing happily with Jack but also watching Joe. Having been at her friend's house for about half an hour she sits on the floor and watches baby Joe crawl past, then she watches him pulling himself up on the couch and standing up. A delighted look crosses her face. She turns to Joe's mummy and says, "He couldn't do that last time." Joe's mummy agrees and says that he has recently started pulling himself up on the furniture and walking around. Elisabeth nods thoughtfully and returns to watching Joe. She watches him crawling around the floor and says, "I used to be able to do that." She then frowns, looks puzzled and says, "No, that's not right I . . ." She frowns again. She is silent for a minute or so, showing only too clearly how intensely she is trying to work something out. Then she says brightly, "When I was bigger I could crawl.'' She frowns again and shakes her head. No, this still isn't it. She frowns in concentration, looks up at mummy's face intently, and then says, "When I was a baby I could do that and now I can't." She smiles with relief. However, a few seconds later it strikes her that this isn't accurate either and she frowns again, shakes her head, but moves off to play. She then decides that she will join in play at being a baby with Jack, and the first thing she does is race off on her hands and knees crawling at a tremendous pace. It is as if this takes her by surprise. She sits back on her bottom, grins broadly and says, "I can crawl now too."

At this point Elisabeth is struggling to understand how quickly her own world has changed, and this is brought home very vividly to her by having a baby sister who is only five months old and an older baby in the room. While she is crawling round she frequently sits to watch her baby sister and then watches Joe. It is clear that she is noticing and observing what her sister does and what the baby of ten months can do. She has come a long way in two years ten months and it is more than she can entirely get a grip on. However what is impressive is her determination to try and understand the changes that have occurred in her young and full life.

The drive to communicate

Emma at two enjoys talking and had been talked to a lot. Her parents try to prepare her for new events. On this occasion Emma's grandma, who is daddy's mother, and who lives abroad, is coming for a visit. On the same day mummy's mother, known as Nanny, is also visiting and she has been a more frequent visitor.

As Emma's mother prepares her for the events of the day, she tells Emma that daddy's mummy will be coming to see them in the morning and mummy's mummy in the afternoon.

These same people, called by different names – names which describe their relationship to Emma's parents, confuse her. "But where is my grandma then?" she asks. "They are both your grandmas," mummy tells her. Emma is delighted. "I've got two, then?", she checks with mummy.

Mum goes on to explain that later grandma will be going home to grandpa. Here the adult flexibility with names is not acceptable to the two year old. Emma wants to get things straight. "No, grandfather," she emphasises, "Grandpa died," (this is accurate, and a recent event). "Nanny lived with grandpa and grandma lives with grandfather." Her accuracy is impressive and the grasp she has on who is related to whom, but she gets confused if grandma is called daddy's mummy and if her mother intermixes grandpa and grandfather. Here we see a little girl who is used to people bothering to communicate with her, now struggling to get the communication right.

The struggle to understand

This same little girl was with her mother sitting quietly in their village church, following the death of mother's father. "Where is grandpa?" Emma asked her mother. Mother had the problem of trying to explain her understanding of death to a two year old. "He's all around us," explained mother. Emma's next comment showed that she couldn't yet manage this abstract idea. "Do you think he's over there?" she asked in a whisper, pointing to a big marble font.

Emma couldn't yet grasp her mother's concept, and if, as mummy explained, grandpa was "all around", then she could only understand this within the limitations of her own experience. It was just a matter of tracking grandpa's whereabouts down. Nonetheless, such explanations are not wasted; in time exposure to abstract ideas will help Emma to move to yet another level of understanding, and her parents continued willingness to explain and discuss, as much as they are able, those new experiences to which she is exposed, encourages Emma to return to those things she cannot yet grasp.

Friends

Children like to meet other children and this is usually managed in the early stages by visits with a grown up, most often mum, to another family. These visits to friends are very important for parents and children. Two year olds are hard work and adults also need the companionship and support of other adults. Some time together is pleasure but too much becomes misery. Parents *and* children need the refreshing experience of mixing with others. This becomes even more important as fewer families live within easy reach of their own extended family.

Most other parents are only too glad of friendly invitations to meet. Some parents, particularly mothers, who have stopped work to be at home with their baby, may have become isolated. It may need an extra effort to discover those other parents in a similar position. Fathers doing a share or all of the child rearing can find this even harder and may need extra encouragement.

These visits to friends with other children are one of the important socialising experiences for the two year old. Here your child has the opportunity to discover about how others live. Even if you take your child to a family of the same class, ethnic or religious background as your own, they won't do everything exactly as you do. All the small details of living will vary.

These differences are a source of richness and interest in our lives but they can also be a source of strain. Parents of young children can be a life-line for each other but can also be a source of rivalry, envy and competition. It helps to know about this in oneself: the wish to have the best, most gifted, most advanced child. But there is also the danger of falling into the opposite extreme, of having the worst child, the most difficult, the one who sleeps the least, the pickiest eater. The danger here is of this becoming a self-fulfilling prophecy.

If your child doesn't talk as much as some of the others, by the time they are four you will have forgotten that someone else's child spoke in sentences weeks before yours, or alternatively that yours did it long before the others! Pleasure in each child's achievements is never a problem. The problem only arises where unfavourable comparisons are made that leave the parents feeling unhappy with the child they've got.

Friends to play

Having friends to play is never all plain sailing for the two year old but it can be mostly fun for parents and children if parents are realistic about what to expect.

Jack and his mother Jane have visitors today. Their friend, Angie, is visiting with her little boy, John, who is a couple of months older than Jack, and a friend's little boy, Matthew, who is only two years and one month. Jack's baby brother is ten months old; he soon joins the other children after his morning nap. Thus we have together three two year olds, Matthew only just passing the two year mark, whilst Jack and his friend John are fast approaching three. The difference in their ages quickly becomes apparent.

After their lunch, Jack and John select two sit-on trucks which are tied together, and take it in turns to pull each other around the room. They talk together in a friendly way, taking it in turns to offer instructions. Matthew stands in the middle of the room, watching them. Matthew's expression changes constantly as he watches the other two boys; at times he joins vicariously in their excitement and when they laugh he laughs. At other moments he looks confused as he tries to follow their game. Matthew makes no attempt to join in and Jack and John do not invite him to do so. When Jack gets off his pull-along truck, Matthew crosses over to inspect it.

After about half an hour Jack and John's friendly play collapses. They have spent some time playing alongside each other with different toys when John begins to play with a toy which actually belongs to Jack's little brother, Joe. Jack suddenly lets up a wail of distress and grabs the toy from John's hand, shouting "Not there, you've got it in the wrong place." John looks confused, takes the toy back from him, and replaces it in the plastic house, where he had had it before. Jack jumps up and down on the spot and begins to cry, saying "It mustn't go there, it's the wrong place, it's the wrong place." He attempts to snatch the toy back from John who hangs on to it for dear life.

Both children's mothers at this point decide that they must intervene. Jack's mother tries quietly to discover what the problem is, but Jack can only keep repeating "It's in the wrong place, it's in the wrong place." His mother explains to him that the little plastic man can fit in any number of places in the house, that the place he had wanted to put it, is where *she* puts it when she's tidying away. Jack insists it must go in *that* place. John meanwhile is trying to grab the toy out of Jack's hand. John's mother comments gently that Jack is a bit upset and says to John that it might help if they listened to what Jack wants to tell them about the house. John says that he wants to put the toy where he wants to put it. Jack is reminded by his mother that actually the toy isn't even his, it's Joe's, his little brother's and anyway they must share. Jack says emphatically, "I don't want to share." His mother decides to take him out of the room to calm him down. They leave and John now has the toy in his hand. He looks at the toy and he looks at the house and then he throws the toy on the floor. Clearly all this bad will around the house has contaminated the toy and the house and now John doesn't want to play with it any more.

Perhaps one of the things this example illustrates is the amount of tact and goodwill needed not only by little children but by their mothers too! It is important not to underestimate the pressure on mothers when their children refuse to play together "in a nice way". It is only too easy either to be embarrassed by one's own child and see the point of view of the other, or to become totally identified with your own child and not to see the impact on another child. It is only quiet and tactful reasoning of the kind that happened in the incident described above that helps children gradually to learn to play together in a more sustained and reasonable way.

Saying goodbye

When it is time to go home John is very tired and has had several grizzly patches shortly before, during which he could not be reasoned with but could only be cuddled. At such times it is only too evident how quickly the maturity of a two year old collapses, they become little babies again when only mother will do, times when mothers have to be exceedingly calm and reasonable.

John doesn't want to go but he equally doesn't want to stay. He doesn't want to put his coat on. He doesn't want to say goodbye. Everything his mother suggests is met with an angry protest and a wail. He struggles as his coat is put on. Fortunately for John his mother seems to understand very clearly that he is tired; she doesn't seem unduly put out by him and doesn't feel persecuted by his behaviour. It is important, of course, to notice that her friend is looking sympathetic and not critical so there is no outside pressure on mother to push John into a conformity, and a coat, that he can't yet manage. He therefore leaves crying, red-faced and refusing to say goodbye. Matthew leaves with them, subdued but waving. Interestingly this doesn't seem to put Jack out unduly who anyway goes to the window and calls out in a friendly way, "Bye John, bye, see you soon."

Things often go wrong at the end of a happy enough period of playing together. Goodbyes are often difficult. As grown-ups we have adult standards of reasonable behaviour at these times – the importance of thanking one's host and so on. Some parents try to insist on this with their two year olds. Perhaps a more helpful model is to "encourage", by example, the two year old towards the behaviour we see as desirable.

During Jack's time with his visitors one of the striking things was the reasonableness of the mothers. Reasonableness is not just good for self preservation but something children imbibe.

Children are sensitive to what is happening around them even when they do not "understand" it. The chances are that a two year old will not understand what he has done wrong – only that he's been "naughty" and made everyone cross.

Playgroups and nursery school

The age at which a child is ready to start playgroup or nursery school varies enormously.

Children with older siblings are often ready sooner for going off into the world on their own. There is already a culture for it; big brother or big sister goes off to school in the morning and is collected later. This gives a tantalising glimpse of the playground and the world of school. Talk around the tea or dinner table about what big brother or sister did at school means that a real picture begins to build up in the two year old's mind. The needs of older siblings means that the two year old will also, at home, have had the experience of fitting in with the hurly burly of family life.

The two year old who is the first in the family doesn't

have this experience. His life experience so far will be different, and nor will the parents have had the experience of leaving a child at a nursery or playgroup. It is wise never to underestimate the impact of this first big separation for the child's mother. It is a very important day – signalling a new point in their lives together. The child is no longer just mum's and dad's baby, but will have separate experiences outside the family. This means that it is essential that parents trust the people to whom they are handing over their child.

Playgroups are commonly run by a playgroup leader plus a rota of parents. It is a culture in which it is usually very easy to stay with your child and/or to leave for just a little while and pop back; to start with just an hour and build up until it is the child who is asking to go to playgroup.

Some nursery schools are run on a similar basis: you can visit with your child, settle him or her in, and start on two mornings or afternoons and gradually build up. Others insist on five mornings or afternoons from the beginning and insist the child is left from the first day. If this is so you need to think very carefully about whether your child is ready for this, since it is the quality of the first experience of being with a group of other children which will influence the child's future attitude to school. If it is fun, if the adults are sensitive and loving, then your child is likely to look on future similar experiences positively. A bad experience early on can put a child off school. So that whilst socialising with other children is important, there are a range of ways in which this can be provided for and the important thing is that it should be enjoyable.

Separating from your child

This is usually the first big separation. Most often it is the mother who has the task of taking her child for the first time to nursery school or playgroup. It stirs up separations the mother herself has had and even if these have largely been negotiated successfully, there is no getting away from the fact that it is an emotional experience. Many mothers confess to crying when they leave their child at school for the first time. So much trust is needed. Trust in the adults you have left your child with, whether they will be kind and understanding, but also trust in your child. Will your child be able to use all you've tried to give them so far to negotiate this new step? Finally of course there is the need for trust in yourself. Have you made the right decision; chosen the right nursery school, and the right time to begin? The rush of emotion most mothers experience is not only feeling for the child but also her own memories at being left.

Jack's mother had many doubts as to starting Jack at nursery when he was two and three quarters. He was the first child in his family so he hadn't seen brother or sister go off to school but nearly all his little friends had started nursery school and Jack's mother was worried that he'd be left behind, missing out on something important in some indefinable way.

On Jack's first morning he was well prepared and seemed keen, having already had a visit with his mother. At mum's suggestion he took a favourite toy with him and at his own suggestion he took a scarf of mum's and a toy belonging to his baby brother. He refused offers of a nice bag to carry them in and insisted on transporting these treasures in a rather tatty carrier bag.

Jack knew his friend would be there too. All was fine at the beginning but when it was time for mother to leave Jack began to cry quietly. Encouraged by the teacher his doubtful mum left a crying Jack behind. Outside school she burst into tears and felt racked with guilt. She felt she'd abandoned Jack, and the couple of hours of school dragged by. When she went to collect him Jack was happy and composed – brandishing a painting in one hand. The teacher confirmed that Jack had been fine. On the way home Jack was not very forthcoming about the content of his morning and was tired and rather grumpy in the afternoon. Jack's mum decided that though it had gone well nevertheless it had still been a strain; something we can still recognise as adults is that new experiences, even if interesting or fun, are still a strain. No doubt too, Jack was also, quite unconsciously, cross with his mother for leaving him, as his rather exacting behaviour in the afternoon seemed to demonstrate.

Jack was going two mornings a week to the nursery school and soon he began to ask if today was the day for school. On his third week Jack was especially keen to get to school. He dressed quickly and rushed ahead of his mother and the push chair with his baby brother in, talking excitedly of meeting Elizabeth at school. Jack was so keen that they arrived early. Jack rushed in, calling out to Elizabeth, only to find that she had not arrived, in fact only a few children had. Jack crumpled, his confidence collapsed, and he burst into tears. This time Jack really cried. Reassurances that Elizabeth would come soon had no impact. Jack's big school boy confidence was not yet firmly established and a disappointment such as this punctured it. Jack's mum had baby Jack on her hands. He needed a lot of cuddling and she had to stay with him for about half an hour before he could cope. Fortunately Jack's mother could give him the time he needed and there was no pressure from Jack's teacher for him to 'be a big boy' before he was ready. Situations such as this, which are very common, need sensitive handling by parents and teachers if a child is to grow in true independence rather than develop a tough veneer.

A few weeks later Jack asked to go to school more often and a third morning was added. Jack's parents were relieved that his first taste of the wider world had gone so well. Perhaps what helped to make this possible was that they had decided that if Jack didn't take to nursery school then they would leave it for six months before trying again.

Jack's first experience of the world outside his family had been negotiated successfully.

FURTHER READING

The Making and Breaking of Affectional Bonds, John Bowlby, Tavistock Publications, 1979

Child's Talk, J.S. Bruner, Norton, 1983

Early Language 'Da-Da', The Developing Child, Peter and Gill de Villiers, Fontana, 1979

The Child, the Family and the Outside World, D.W. Winnicott, Penguin Books, 1964

HELPFUL ORGANISATIONS

Under-Fives Counselling Service, Tavistock Clinic, 120 Belsize Lane, London NW3 5BA (Tel 071 435 7111)

In conjunction with the Child Psychotherapy Trust:

> CRY-sis (Tel 071 404 5011
>
> Parentline (Tel 0268 757 077)
>
> Exploring Parenthood, Latimer Education Centre, 194 Freston Road, London W10 6TT. Parents Advice Line 081 960 1678 (from 10.a.m. to 4.p.m.)

The Pre-School Playgroups Association, 61–63 King's Cross Road, London, WC1X 9LL (Tel 071 833 0991)

Nursery and Pre-School Information Line, PO Box RB, London W1A 4RB (Tel 0874 638007)

Gingerbread Association for One Parent Families., 35 Wellington Street, London WC2 (Tel 071 240 0953)

UNDERSTANDING YOUR CHILD

ORDER FORM FOR TITLES IN THIS SERIES

Send to: Rosendale Press Ltd, Premier House,
10 Greycoat Place, London SW1P 1SB

Price per volume: £4.75 inc post & packing

Understanding Your Baby by Lisa Miller . . . . . copies

Understanding Your 1 Year Old by Deborah Steiner . . . . . copies

Understanding Your 2 Year Old by Susan Reid . . . . . copies

Understanding Your 3 Year Old by Judith Trowell . . . . . copies

Understanding Your 4 Year Old by Lisa Miller . . . . . copies

Understanding Your 5 Year Old by Lesley Holditch . . . . . copies

Further titles in this series in preparation from: Understanding Your
6 Year Old to Understanding Your Teenager

Total amount enclosed: £. . . . .

Name . . . .

Address . . . .

. . . . Post code . . . .